Radical Forgiveness

How to Let Go of Anger and Resentment

Ramchandra

Table of contents:

Understanding the Power of Forgiveness

Forgiveness is a powerful tool that has the ability to transform lives. It allows us to let go of negative emotions such as anger and resentment, and move towards a more positive and fulfilling life. In this chapter, we will explore the power of forgiveness and the benefits it can bring.

First, it's important to understand what forgiveness really means. Forgiveness is not about condoning or excusing someone's actions. Instead, it's about letting go of the negative emotions that are associated with the hurt that someone has caused us. When we forgive, we release ourselves from the burden of anger, resentment, and bitterness. It doesn't mean we forget what happened, but rather we choose to no longer hold on to the negative emotions that are associated with it.

The act of forgiveness has been scientifically proven to have numerous benefits for our mental and physical health. Studies have shown that forgiveness can reduce symptoms of depression, anxiety, and stress. It also leads to better sleep, improved relationships, and a greater sense of well-being.

When we hold on to negative emotions such as anger and resentment, it can lead to a build-up of stress in our bodies. This stress can have negative effects on our physical health, such as increased blood pressure and a weakened immune system. By forgiving and letting go of these negative emotions, we can reduce this stress and improve our overall health.

In addition to the physical benefits, forgiveness can also have a positive impact on our relationships. When we hold grudges and harbour negative emotions towards others, it can create tension and conflict in our relationships. By forgiving, we can create space for healing and reconciliation in our relationships.

Forgiveness also has the power to transform us as individuals. When we forgive, we let go of the negative emotions that are holding us back and create space for growth and personal development. It allows us to move towards a more positive and fulfilling life.

But forgiveness is not always easy. It can be a difficult and painful process, especially when we have been deeply hurt by someone. However, it's important to remember that forgiveness is a choice. We have the power to choose whether or not to hold on to negative emotions or to let them go.

One of the first steps towards forgiveness is acknowledging the pain that has been caused. It's important to allow ourselves to feel the emotions associated with the hurt and to acknowledge how it has affected us. This can be a difficult process, but it's a necessary step towards healing.

It's also important to recognize that forgiveness is a process, and it may take time. It's not something that can be forced or rushed. It's important to allow ourselves the time and space we need to work through our emotions and to come to a place of forgiveness.

Another important aspect of forgiveness is empathy. Empathy is the ability to put ourselves in someone else's shoes and to understand their perspective. When we can empathize with someone who has hurt us, it can create space for forgiveness and healing.

In some cases, forgiveness may not be possible or appropriate. It's important to recognize our own boundaries and to respect our own needs. Sometimes, it may be necessary to remove ourselves from a situation or relationship that is causing us harm.

Ultimately, forgiveness is a powerful tool that has the ability to transform our lives. It allows us to let go of negative emotions and to move towards a more positive and fulfilling life. By choosing to forgive, we can create space for healing, growth, and personal development.

The Root Causes of Anger and Resentment

Anger and resentment are emotions that can be incredibly challenging to deal with. They can create a great deal of stress and tension in our lives, and if left unaddressed, they can have negative consequences for our mental and physical health. In this chapter, we will explore the root causes of anger and resentment, and how we can work to overcome them.

One of the primary causes of anger and resentment is unmet expectations. When we have certain expectations for how things should be, and those expectations are not met, it can lead to feelings of anger and resentment. This can happen in any area of our lives, whether it's in our personal relationships, our careers, or even with ourselves. For example, if we expect our partner to behave a certain way and they don't meet those expectations, we may feel angry or resentful towards them.

Another root cause of anger and resentment is feeling powerless. When we feel like we don't have control over a situation, it can lead to feelings of frustration and anger. This can be particularly challenging in situations where we feel like we've been wronged or treated unfairly. For example, if we've been passed over for a promotion at work, we may feel angry and resentful towards our boss or the company.

Lack of communication is another common cause of anger and resentment. When we feel like our needs are not being heard or understood, it can lead to frustration and anger.

This can happen in any type of relationship, whether it's with a partner, a friend, or a co-worker. For example, if we feel like our boss is not listening to our concerns about a project, we may feel angry and resentful towards them.

Past experiences can also be a root cause of anger and resentment. When we've been hurt in the past, it can be difficult to let go of those negative emotions. This can lead to feelings of anger and resentment towards the person who hurt us, even if they're no longer in our lives. For example, if we were bullied in high school, we may still feel angry and resentful towards the people who bullied us, even years later.

Finally, a lack of self-awareness can also contribute to feelings of anger and resentment. When we're not in tune with our own emotions and needs, it can be challenging to manage our anger and resentment. For example, if we're feeling stressed and overwhelmed, we may lash out at our loved ones without realizing that we're projecting our own feelings onto them.

So, how can we work to overcome these root causes of anger and resentment? The first step is to identify the source of our anger and resentment. This may involve some self-reflection and introspection. Once we've identified the root cause, we can work to address it directly. For example, if we're feeling powerless in a situation, we may need to work on building our own sense of agency and control.

Effective communication is also key to managing anger and resentment. When we're able to express our needs and concerns clearly and effectively, we can reduce the likelihood of misunderstandings and conflicts. This may involve learning new communication skills or seeking the help of a therapist or counsellor.

Working on forgiveness is another important step towards overcoming anger and resentment. When we're able to forgive others for their mistakes and shortcomings, we can release ourselves from the negative emotions that are holding us back. This doesn't mean we have to forget what happened, but it does mean we're choosing to no longer hold onto the negative emotions associated with it.

The Consequences of Holding on to Grudges

Holding onto grudges can have significant consequences for our mental and physical health, as well as our relationships with others. In this chapter, we will explore some of the consequences of holding onto grudges and how we can work to let them go.

One of the most significant consequences of holding onto grudges is the impact it can have on our mental health. When we hold onto negative emotions such as anger and resentment, it can lead to increased stress and anxiety. This, in turn, can lead to a variety of physical symptoms such as headaches, muscle tension, and fatigue. Over time, this can have a significant impact on our overall wellbeing and quality of life.

Holding onto grudges can also impact our relationships with others. When we're holding onto anger and resentment, it can create tension and conflict in our relationships. We may find ourselves constantly arguing or avoiding certain people altogether. This can lead to feelings of loneliness and isolation, which can further impact our mental health.

Another consequence of holding onto grudges is that it can prevent us from moving forward in our lives. When we're constantly focused on the past, it can be difficult to focus on the present and plan for the future. This can lead to missed opportunities and a sense of stagnation in our lives. Additionally, it can prevent us from experiencing joy and happiness in the present moment.

One of the most significant consequences of holding onto grudges is that it can prevent us from experiencing forgiveness. When we're holding onto negative emotions towards someone, it can be challenging to forgive them for their actions. Forgiveness is a crucial component of moving forward and letting go of negative emotions. Without forgiveness, we may find ourselves stuck in a cycle of anger and resentment, unable to move on from past hurts.

So, how can we work to let go of grudges and move towards forgiveness? The first step is to recognize the negative impact that holding onto grudges is having on our lives. This may involve some self-reflection and introspection. We may need to acknowledge the role that we've played in perpetuating the cycle of anger and resentment.

Once we've recognized the negative impact of holding onto grudges, we can work to actively let them go. This may involve forgiveness practices such as meditation or writing letters to those who have hurt us. It may also involve seeking the help of a therapist or counsellor to work through our emotions.

Another important step towards letting go of grudges is to focus on the present moment. This may involve mindfulness practices such as meditation or journaling. When we're able to focus on the present moment, we can let go of the past and move towards a more positive future.

Finally, it's important to focus on building positive relationships with others. When we're able to build positive relationships, we're less likely to hold onto grudges and negative emotions. This may involve working on our communication skills, practicing empathy and compassion, and actively seeking out opportunities to connect with others.

In conclusion, holding onto grudges can have significant consequences for our mental and physical health, as well as our relationships with others. However, by recognizing the negative impact of holding onto grudges and actively working to let them go, we can move towards forgiveness and a more positive future. It may take time and effort, but the rewards of letting go of grudges are well worth it.

The Science behind Forgiveness

Forgiveness is a complex process that involves both cognitive and emotional factors. In this chapter, we will explore the science behind forgiveness and how it can help us to let go of anger and resentment.

Research has shown that forgiveness is associated with a range of positive outcomes, including improved mental and physical health, increased well-being, and better interpersonal relationships. Studies have also suggested that forgiveness can reduce stress and anxiety, lower blood pressure, and even boost the immune system.

One of the key components of forgiveness is empathy. Empathy is the ability to understand and share the feelings of others. When we're able to empathize with someone who has hurt us, we're more likely to be able to forgive them. This is because empathy helps us to see the situation from their perspective and to understand the factors that may have led to their actions.

Another important factor in forgiveness is cognitive reappraisal. Cognitive reappraisal involves changing the way we think about a situation or event. When we're able to reframe the situation in a more positive light, we're more likely to be able to forgive those who have hurt us. For example, we may reframe the situation as a learning experience or an opportunity for growth.

Research has also suggested that forgiveness is linked to increased activity in the prefrontal cortex, the part of the brain that is responsible for decision-making and emotional regulation. This suggests that forgiveness may be a cognitive process that involves the deliberate choice to let go of negative emotions and to move towards a more positive outlook.

In addition to the cognitive processes involved in forgiveness, there are also emotional processes at play. Forgiveness involves a shift in emotional response, from anger and resentment to empathy and compassion. This shift is often accompanied by a sense of relief and a release of negative emotions.

One theory that has been proposed to explain the emotional processes involved in forgiveness is the "affect infusion model". According to this model, forgiveness involves the infusion of positive affect, or emotion, into the memory of the hurtful event. This positive affect can then overwrite the negative emotions associated with the event, leading to forgiveness.

There are also cultural and social factors that can influence forgiveness. Research has suggested that cultural factors such as individualism vs. collectivism, religiosity, and social support can impact the likelihood and effectiveness of forgiveness.

One of the most important things to understand about forgiveness is that it's a process, not a one-time event. Forgiveness requires ongoing effort and practice, and it's not always easy. It may involve confronting difficult emotions and working through complex issues. However, the benefits of forgiveness are well worth the effort.

So, how can we work to cultivate forgiveness in our lives? One important step is to practice empathy and compassion towards others. This may involve trying to understand the motivations behind someone's hurtful actions or considering the larger context in which the situation occurred.

Another important step is to work on cognitive reappraisal. This may involve reframing the situation in a more positive light or trying to find the silver lining in a difficult situation.

Finally, it's important to practice self-forgiveness. When we're able to forgive ourselves for our mistakes and shortcomings, we're more likely to be able to extend forgiveness to others.

In conclusion, forgiveness is a complex process that involves both cognitive and emotional factors. However, by understanding the science behind forgiveness and working to cultivate empathy, cognitive reappraisal, and self-forgiveness, we can let go of anger and resentment and move towards a more positive future.

The Art of Letting Go

Letting go of anger and resentment is a vital part of the forgiveness process. Holding onto negative emotions can be incredibly damaging to our mental and physical health, and it can prevent us from moving forward and living our best lives. In this chapter, we'll explore the art of letting go and how it can help us to forgive and move on from past hurts.

The first step in letting go is to acknowledge our feelings. It's important to allow ourselves to feel the full range of emotions that come with being hurt or wronged. This may involve expressing our feelings through journaling, talking to a trusted friend or therapist, or engaging in physical activity to release pent-up emotions.

Once we've acknowledged our feelings, we can begin to work on letting them go. This may involve identifying the thoughts or beliefs that are contributing to our negative emotions and challenging them. For example, we may be holding onto resentment because we believe that the person who hurt us should have known better, or that they should be punished for their actions. By challenging these thoughts and beliefs, we can begin to shift our perspective and let go of our negative emotions.

Another important aspect of letting go is acceptance. Acceptance involves acknowledging that we can't change the past and that we can't control the actions of others. When we're able to accept this reality, we can begin to let go of our attachment to the situation and move towards a more positive future.

One useful technique for letting go is mindfulness. Mindfulness involves being present in the moment and observing our thoughts and emotions without judgment. By practicing mindfulness, we can become more aware of our negative thought patterns and learn to detach from them. This can help us to let go of negative emotions and move towards a more peaceful and positive mind-set.

Another helpful technique for letting go is gratitude. Gratitude involves focusing on the positive aspects of our lives and expressing gratitude for the good things that we have. By practicing gratitude, we can shift our focus away from our negative emotions and towards the positive aspects of our lives. This can help us to let go of anger and resentment and cultivate a more positive outlook.

It's also important to recognize that letting go is a process, not a one-time event. It may take time and effort to release negative emotions and move towards forgiveness. However, by practicing self-compassion and self-care, we can support ourselves through the process of letting go and create a more positive future for ourselves.

In conclusion, letting go is an essential part of the forgiveness process. By acknowledging our emotions, challenging negative thought patterns, accepting reality, and practicing mindfulness and gratitude, we can let go of anger and resentment and move towards a more positive future. Remember that letting go is a process, and be gentle with yourself as you work towards forgiveness and healing. With time and effort, you can cultivate the art of letting go and create a more peaceful and fulfilling life.

The Role of Empathy in Forgiveness

Empathy is a key component of forgiveness. It involves putting ourselves in someone else's shoes and trying to understand their thoughts, feelings, and motivations. When we're able to empathize with someone who has hurt us, it can help us to see things from their perspective and begin to let go of our anger and resentment. In this chapter, we'll explore the role of empathy in forgiveness and how we can cultivate empathy as a tool for healing.

Empathy allows us to connect with others on a deeper level and to understand their experiences and perspectives. When we're able to empathize with someone who has hurt us, it can help us to see them as human beings with their own struggles, fears, and vulnerabilities. This can create a sense of connection and compassion that can be essential in the forgiveness process.

One of the challenges of empathy is that it can be difficult to empathize with someone who has hurt us. Our natural instinct may be to distance ourselves from them or to view them as "the enemy." However, when we're able to push past this initial reaction and see things from their perspective, it can be a powerful tool for healing.

One way to cultivate empathy is to practice active listening. This involves giving someone our full attention and really listening to what they have to say. When we're able to listen without judgment and without interrupting, it can create a sense of trust and safety that can allow for deeper understanding and empathy.

Another way to cultivate empathy is to practice putting ourselves in someone else's shoes. This may involve imagining what it would be like to be in their situation, or reflecting on times when we may have acted in a hurtful or thoughtless way ourselves. When we're able to see things from someone else's perspective, it can create a sense of empathy and understanding that can be essential in the forgiveness process.

It's important to note that empathy does not mean condoning or excusing someone's hurtful behaviour. Rather, it involves trying to understand the factors that may have led to their actions and acknowledging the pain that they may be experiencing as well.

In the forgiveness process, empathy can help to break down barriers and create a sense of connection and compassion between ourselves and the person who has hurt us. When we're able to empathize with their experiences and perspectives, it can create a space for healing and growth.

In conclusion, empathy is a vital tool in the forgiveness process. By cultivating empathy through active listening, putting ourselves in someone else's shoes, and acknowledging the pain that both parties may be experiencing, we can begin to let go of anger and resentment and move towards a more compassionate and connected future. Remember that empathy is a skill that can be developed over time, and be gentle with yourself as you work towards forgiveness and healing. With time and effort, you can cultivate the role of empathy in your life and create a more peaceful and fulfilling future.

The Importance of Self-Forgiveness

Self-forgiveness is a vital component of the forgiveness process, and it involves letting go of anger and resentment towards oneself. When we're able to forgive ourselves for past mistakes and shortcomings, we can experience a sense of relief and move forward towards a more positive future. In this chapter, we'll explore the importance of self-forgiveness and how we can cultivate it in our lives.

Many of us carry feelings of guilt and shame over past mistakes and shortcomings. We may hold onto these negative emotions, believing that they somehow make up for our past transgressions. However, the truth is that holding onto anger and resentment towards ourselves can be damaging to our mental and emotional well-being. It can lead to feelings of self-doubt, low self-esteem, and even depression.

One of the challenges of self-forgiveness is that it can be difficult to let go of these negative emotions. We may feel that we don't deserve forgiveness or that we're somehow unworthy of it. However, the truth is that self-forgiveness is an essential component of personal growth and healing.

To begin the process of self-forgiveness, it's important to acknowledge and accept responsibility for our past mistakes and shortcomings. This involves acknowledging the pain that we may have caused ourselves and others, and taking steps to make amends and learn from our mistakes.

Another key component of self-forgiveness is self-compassion. This involves treating ourselves with kindness and understanding, just as we would treat a friend or loved one. We can practice self-compassion by acknowledging our emotions, being gentle with ourselves, and reframing negative self-talk into positive affirmations.

In addition to self-compassion, it's important to practice self-care. This involves taking care of our physical, emotional, and spiritual well-being through activities such as exercise, meditation, and spending time with loved ones.

It's also important to cultivate a sense of self-awareness and self-reflection. This involves taking the time to reflect on our past actions and decisions, and considering how we can make positive changes in the future. By engaging in self-reflection, we can gain a deeper understanding of ourselves and our motivations, and move towards a more fulfilling and positive future.

In conclusion, self-forgiveness is an essential component of personal growth and healing. By acknowledging our past mistakes and shortcomings, practicing self-compassion and self-care, and engaging in self-reflection, we can let go of anger and resentment towards ourselves and move towards a more positive future. Remember that self-forgiveness is a process that takes time and effort, and be gentle with yourself as you work towards forgiveness and healing. With time and effort, you can cultivate self-forgiveness in your life and create a more peaceful and fulfilling future.

Moving Beyond Blame: Taking Responsibility for Your Emotions

Blaming others for our negative emotions is a common human behaviour. We may blame our partners, parents, co-workers, or even strangers for making us angry or upset. However, blaming others only serves to perpetuate negative emotions and prevent us from finding true peace and happiness. In this chapter, we'll explore how taking responsibility for our emotions can help us move beyond blame and cultivate a more positive mind-set.

When we blame others for our negative emotions, we give away our power and agency. We allow external factors to control our emotions and prevent us from taking control of our lives. However, by taking responsibility for our emotions, we reclaim our power and can begin to cultivate a more positive and fulfilling life.

One of the key steps in taking responsibility for our emotions is to acknowledge and accept our feelings. This involves recognizing when we're feeling angry, upset, or hurt, and allowing ourselves to experience those emotions without judgment or resistance. By accepting our emotions, we can begin to understand the underlying causes and take steps to address them.

Another important aspect of taking responsibility for our emotions is to recognize that our feelings are not caused by external factors. While other people or events may trigger our emotions, it's ultimately our interpretation and response to those events that determines how we feel. By taking ownership of our emotions, we can recognize that we have the power to choose our responses and create a more positive outcome.

One effective technique for taking responsibility for our emotions is to practice mindfulness. Mindfulness involves paying attention to the present moment, without judgment or distraction. By practicing mindfulness, we can observe our thoughts and emotions without becoming attached to them, and choose how we respond in a more intentional and positive way.

Another important aspect of taking responsibility for our emotions is to communicate our feelings to others in a constructive way. This involves expressing our emotions in a way that is respectful, honest, and non-judgmental. By communicating our feelings in this way, we can create deeper connections with others and work towards resolving conflicts in a more positive way.

In conclusion, taking responsibility for our emotions is a key step in moving beyond blame and cultivating a more positive mind-set. By acknowledging and accepting our emotions, recognizing that our feelings are not caused by external factors, practicing mindfulness, and communicating our feelings in a constructive way, we can take control of our lives and create a more peaceful and fulfilling future. Remember that taking responsibility for our emotions is a process that takes time and effort, and be gentle with yourself as you work towards cultivating a more positive mind-set. With time and effort, you can move beyond blame and create a more fulfilling and positive life.

The Benefits of Forgiveness for Mental Health

Forgiveness is a powerful tool that can have significant benefits for our mental health. When we hold onto anger, resentment, and other negative emotions, we can experience a range of mental health issues, including anxiety, depression, and stress. In this chapter, we'll explore the ways in which forgiveness can improve our mental health and wellbeing.

One of the key benefits of forgiveness is that it can help to reduce stress and anxiety. When we hold onto grudges and negative emotions, our bodies release stress hormones like cortisol, which can lead to physical and mental health problems. By forgiving others and letting go of our anger and resentment, we can reduce the amount of stress and anxiety we experience and promote a more positive state of mind.

Forgiveness can also help to improve our relationships with others. When we hold onto anger and resentment, it can create a barrier between us and the people around us. By forgiving others, we can build stronger connections with the people in our lives and promote a sense of trust and understanding. This can lead to greater happiness, satisfaction, and fulfilment in our relationships.

Another important benefit of forgiveness is that it can improve our self-esteem and self-worth. When we hold onto grudges and negative emotions, we can begin to feel like victims and lose our sense of agency and control. By forgiving others and taking control of our emotions, we can restore our sense of self-worth and promote a more positive self-image.

Forgiveness can also help to promote a more positive outlook on life. When we hold onto anger and resentment, it can colour our perception of the world and prevent us from seeing the positive things in life. By forgiving others and letting go of negative emotions, we can begin to focus on the good things in life and promote a more optimistic mind-set.

Finally, forgiveness can help us to heal from past traumas and move on from difficult experiences. When we hold onto anger and resentment, it can keep us trapped in the past and prevent us from moving forward. By forgiving others and ourselves, we can let go of the past and begin to create a more positive and fulfilling future.

In conclusion, forgiveness can have a range of benefits for our mental health and wellbeing. By reducing stress and anxiety, improving our relationships with others, promoting a more positive self-image, enhancing our outlook on life, and promoting healing and growth, forgiveness can help us to create a more fulfilling and satisfying life. Remember that forgiveness is a process that takes time and effort, and be gentle with yourself as you work towards cultivating a more forgiving mind-set. With time and effort, you can reap the benefits of forgiveness and create a more positive and fulfilling future for yourself.

Strategies for Cultivating Forgiveness

Forgiveness can be a difficult process, especially when we've been hurt deeply by others. However, it is possible to cultivate forgiveness with the right strategies and mind-set. In this chapter, we'll explore some effective strategies for cultivating forgiveness and letting go of anger and resentment.

Practice empathy: One of the most important strategies for cultivating forgiveness is practicing empathy. Empathy involves putting yourself in the other person's shoes and trying to understand their perspective. When we can see things from another person's point of view, we can begin to let go of anger and resentment and move towards forgiveness.

Accept responsibility for your emotions: Another important strategy for cultivating forgiveness is accepting responsibility for your emotions. This involves recognizing that you are the one who is holding onto anger and resentment, and that you have the power to let it go. By accepting responsibility for your emotions, you can take control of the forgiveness process and move towards a more positive mind-set.

Focus on the present moment: It's easy to get caught up in the past when we've been hurt by others. However, focusing on the present moment can help us to let go of negative emotions and move towards forgiveness. Practice mindfulness meditation or other techniques that help you to stay present and focused on the here and now.

Practice self-compassion: Forgiving others can be difficult, but it's even more difficult to forgive ourselves. However, practicing self-compassion can help us to let go of self-blame and move towards self-forgiveness. Treat yourself with kindness and understanding, and remind yourself that everyone makes mistakes.

Seek support: Forgiveness can be a challenging process, and it's important to seek support from others when you're struggling. Talk to friends, family members, or a therapist about your feelings and experiences. They can provide a listening ear and offer helpful advice for moving towards forgiveness.

Reframe your perspective: Sometimes, it can be helpful to reframe our perspective on a situation in order to let go of negative emotions. Ask yourself: what can I learn from this experience? How can I grow and become a better person as a result of this situation? By reframing your perspective, you can begin to see the situation in a more positive light and move towards forgiveness.

Practice forgiveness rituals: Forgiveness rituals can be helpful for letting go of negative emotions and moving towards forgiveness. This can include writing a letter to the person who hurt you (even if you don't send it), lighting a candle, or performing a symbolic act that represents letting go of negative emotions.

In conclusion, cultivating forgiveness can be a challenging process, but it is possible with the right strategies and mind-set. Practice empathy, accept responsibility for your emotions, focus on the present moment, practice self-compassion, seek support, reframe your perspective, and practice forgiveness rituals to let go of anger and resentment and move towards a more positive and fulfilling future. Remember that forgiveness is a process that takes time and effort, and be gentle with yourself as you work towards cultivating a more forgiving mind-set. With time and effort, you can reap the benefits of forgiveness and create a more positive and fulfilling life for yourself.

The Power of Gratitude in the Forgiveness Process

Gratitude is a powerful emotion that can have a profound impact on our mental and emotional wellbeing. In the forgiveness process, cultivating a sense of gratitude can help us to let go of anger and resentment and move towards a more positive and forgiving mind-set. In this chapter, we'll explore the power of gratitude in the forgiveness process and how to cultivate a sense of gratitude in your own life.

Gratitude shifts your focus: When we're holding onto anger and resentment, our focus is often on the negative aspects of a situation or person. However, gratitude can help to shift our focus towards the positive aspects of our lives. By cultivating a sense of gratitude, we can begin to see the good in people and situations, even in difficult times.

Gratitude reduces stress: Holding onto anger and resentment can be stressful and exhausting. However, gratitude has been shown to reduce stress levels and improve our overall sense of wellbeing. When we focus on the things we're grateful for, we can experience a sense of calm and peace.

Gratitude promotes forgiveness: When we're grateful for the positive aspects of a situation or person, it becomes easier to let go of negative emotions and move towards forgiveness. By focusing on what we're grateful for, we can shift our mind-set towards a more positive and forgiving perspective.

Gratitude helps us to see the bigger picture: When we're stuck in anger and resentment, it can be difficult to see the bigger picture. However, cultivating a sense of gratitude can help us to see things from a broader perspective. We can see how our experiences and relationships have shaped us into the person we are today, and we can appreciate the lessons we've learned along the way.

Gratitude fosters empathy: When we're grateful for the positive aspects of a person or situation, it becomes easier to understand their perspective and empathize with them. By practicing gratitude, we can foster empathy and compassion, which are essential components of the forgiveness process.

So, how can you cultivate a sense of gratitude in your own life? Here are some tips:

Keep a gratitude journal: Write down three things you're grateful for every day. This can be anything from a good cup of coffee to a supportive friend or family member.

Practice mindfulness: Take a few minutes each day to focus on the present moment and appreciate the things around you. This can be as simple as taking a few deep breaths and noticing the beauty of nature.

Say "thank you": Express gratitude to the people around you. Say "thank you" to a friend who has helped you, or to a co-worker who has gone above and beyond.

Volunteer: Volunteering is a great way to cultivate gratitude and give back to your community. Helping others can give you a sense of purpose and gratitude.

Practice forgiveness: Forgiving others can be difficult, but it's an essential component of cultivating gratitude. By forgiving others, we can let go of anger and resentment and focus on the positive aspects of our relationships and experiences.

In conclusion, cultivating a sense of gratitude is an essential component of the forgiveness process. Gratitude can help us to shift our focus towards the positive aspects of our lives, reduce stress, promote forgiveness, help us to see the bigger picture, and foster empathy. By keeping a gratitude journal, practicing mindfulness, saying "thank you," volunteering, and practicing forgiveness, you can cultivate a sense of gratitude in your own life and move towards a more positive and forgiving mind-set. Remember that forgiveness is a process that takes time and effort, but with gratitude, it is possible to let go of anger and resentment and create a more fulfilling life for yourself.

The Role of Mindfulness in Letting Go of Resentment

Mindfulness can be a powerful tool for cultivating forgiveness and letting go of resentment. It involves bringing your attention to the present moment and accepting your thoughts and emotions without judgment. In this chapter, we will explore the role of mindfulness in the forgiveness process and provide some practical tips for incorporating mindfulness practices into your daily life.

One of the primary benefits of mindfulness in the forgiveness process is that it allows you to become more aware of your thoughts and emotions. Often, we hold onto anger and resentment because we are caught up in negative thought patterns and we are not fully aware of how our emotions are impacting us. By practicing mindfulness, you can develop a greater awareness of your thoughts and emotions, which can help you to identify patterns of thinking that are contributing to your resentment.

Another benefit of mindfulness in the forgiveness process is that it helps you to develop a more compassionate and accepting attitude towards yourself and others. When you are mindful, you are better able to observe your thoughts and emotions without judging them as good or bad. This can help you to develop greater empathy for others and to let go of the blame and judgment that can contribute to resentment.

Here are some practical tips for incorporating mindfulness practices into your daily life:

Start with a daily meditation practice: Meditation is a powerful tool for developing mindfulness. Set aside some time each day to sit quietly and focus on your breath. As thoughts and emotions arise, simply observe them without judgment and bring your attention back to your breath.

Practice mindful breathing: When you feel yourself becoming angry or resentful, take a few deep breaths and focus your attention on your breath. This can help to calm your mind and body and bring you back to the present moment.

Practice mindful listening: When you are in a conversation with someone, try to give them your full attention. Listen to what they are saying without judgment and without thinking about what you are going to say next.

Practice mindful eating: When you are eating a meal, take the time to savour each bite and fully appreciate the flavours and textures of your food. This can help you to develop a greater appreciation for the simple pleasures in life.

Practice gratitude: Each day, take some time to reflect on the things in your life that you are grateful for. This can help you to develop a more positive outlook and to let go of negative emotions.

In conclusion, mindfulness can be a powerful tool for cultivating forgiveness and letting go of resentment. By developing a greater awareness of your thoughts and emotions and cultivating a more compassionate and accepting attitude towards yourself and others, you can begin to break free from the negative thought patterns and emotions that are contributing to your resentment. With consistent practice, mindfulness can help you to develop a greater sense of peace and well-being, and to live a more fulfilling and meaningful life.

How to Practice Forgiveness in Daily Life

In order to truly let go of anger and resentment, forgiveness must become a daily practice. This means consciously choosing forgiveness as a way of life and applying forgiveness principles to all areas of your life. Here are some strategies for practicing forgiveness in daily life:

Start with yourself: The first step to practicing forgiveness is to forgive yourself. Recognize that you are not perfect and that you will make mistakes. Be kind to yourself and show yourself the same compassion you would show a friend.

Cultivate empathy: Make a conscious effort to put yourself in someone else's shoes. This will help you to understand their perspective and to see things from their point of view. This will make it easier to forgive them.

Practice gratitude: Gratitude is a powerful tool for forgiveness. Take time each day to reflect on the things you are grateful for. This will help you to focus on the positive and to let go of negative emotions.

Let go of blame: Blaming others for your problems will only make things worse. Take responsibility for your actions and let go of blame. This will help you to move forward and to forgive others.

Practice mindfulness: Mindfulness is the practice of being present in the moment. This can help you to let go of negative thoughts and emotions and to focus on the present moment. Mindfulness can also help you to cultivate compassion and empathy.

Use affirmations: Affirmations are positive statements that you repeat to yourself. Use affirmations to remind yourself that you are capable of forgiveness and that you are worthy of forgiveness.

Communicate effectively: Effective communication is essential for practicing forgiveness. Learn how to communicate your feelings and needs in a clear and compassionate way. This will help you to resolve conflicts and to forgive others.

Practice self-care: Practicing self-care is essential for forgiveness. Take time to take care of yourself physically, emotionally, and mentally. This will help you to feel better and to be more open to forgiveness.

Set boundaries: Setting healthy boundaries is essential for forgiveness. Learn how to say no and how to protect yourself from people who are not healthy for you. This will help you to create a space for forgiveness in your life.

Practice forgiveness daily: Forgiveness is a daily practice. Make a conscious effort to practice forgiveness every day. This can be as simple as forgiving someone who cuts you off in traffic or as complex as forgiving a family member for a past hurt. The more you practice forgiveness, the easier it will become.

In conclusion, forgiveness is a process that requires practice and patience. By using these strategies to practice forgiveness in your daily life, you can learn to let go of anger and resentment and to create a more peaceful and fulfilling life. Remember, forgiveness is a choice that you make for yourself, and it is never too late to start practicing.

The Importance of Boundaries in the Forgiveness Process

Forgiveness does not mean that you have to tolerate unacceptable behaviour or allow someone to continue hurting you. Setting boundaries is an essential part of the forgiveness process, and it involves creating healthy limits for yourself and others. Boundaries help to protect your emotional, physical, and mental well-being while ensuring that you treat others with respect and kindness.

When we experience hurt or betrayal, it can be challenging to trust again. Setting boundaries can help rebuild trust in relationships while also ensuring that you don't become a victim of further harm. Boundaries allow you to communicate your needs and expectations clearly, which can prevent misunderstandings and hurt feelings.

Boundaries also help to establish mutual respect in relationships. By communicating your boundaries, you are showing that you value yourself and your needs, which can lead to healthier and more fulfilling relationships. When we have healthy boundaries, we are less likely to feel resentful, angry, or frustrated.

However, setting boundaries can be challenging, especially if we have not done so in the past. It can be challenging to communicate your needs without feeling guilty or ashamed, and it can be challenging to stand up for yourself without feeling confrontational.

Here are some tips for setting healthy boundaries:

Identify your values and needs: Before setting boundaries, take some time to identify your values and needs. What is most important to you? What do you need in your relationships to feel happy and fulfilled? Once you have a clear understanding of your values and needs, it will be easier to communicate them to others.

Be clear and specific: When communicating your boundaries, be clear and specific about what you need. Use "I" statements to express your feelings, and be specific about the behaviours or actions that are not acceptable.

Practice self-compassion: Setting boundaries can be challenging, and its okay to make mistakes. Be gentle with yourself and remember that it's okay to ask for what you need.

Consider the consequences: Before setting a boundary, consider the potential consequences. Will the boundary negatively impact the relationship? Are there alternative ways to communicate your needs?

Enforce your boundaries: Once you have set a boundary, it's important to enforce it. If someone violates your boundary, calmly and assertively communicate your feelings and reinforce the boundary.

Seek support: Setting boundaries can be challenging, especially if you have a history of being a people-pleaser. Seek support from a therapist, trusted friend, or support group.

In conclusion, boundaries are an essential part of the forgiveness process. They allow us to communicate our needs and expectations while ensuring that we treat others with respect and kindness. Setting healthy boundaries can help rebuild trust in relationships and prevent further harm, leading to healthier and more fulfilling relationships. Remember to be clear and specific, practice self-compassion, consider the consequences, enforce your boundaries, and seek support when needed.

Emotional wounds can be deeply ingrained in us and often manifest as negative energy that can disrupt our lives, relationships, and overall well-being. However, the good news is that it's possible to release this negative energy and heal our emotional wounds through forgiveness.

When we hold onto anger, resentment, and grudges, we are essentially holding onto negative energy that can weigh us down and prevent us from moving forward. This negative energy can also have physical consequences, such as increased stress levels, weakened immune system, and even chronic pain.

The first step in releasing negative energy and healing emotional wounds is to acknowledge that we are holding onto these negative emotions. We must be willing to take responsibility for our emotions and recognize that we have the power to choose how we respond to situations.

Once we have acknowledged our negative emotions, the next step is to forgive ourselves and others involved. This can be a challenging process, but it is essential for releasing negative energy and promoting emotional healing.

When forgiving others, it's important to recognize that forgiveness does not mean condoning the actions of others or denying the harm that has been caused. It simply means letting go of the negative emotions associated with the situation and choosing to move forward.

Forgiving ourselves can also be a difficult process, especially if we have held onto self-blame or guilt. However, self-forgiveness is crucial for releasing negative energy and promoting emotional healing. We must be kind and compassionate with ourselves, recognizing that we are human and capable of making mistakes.

In addition to forgiveness, there are other practices that can help us release negative energy and heal emotional wounds. These include:

Meditation: Meditation can help us calm our minds and release negative emotions. By focusing on our breath and letting go of negative thoughts, we can promote emotional healing and overall well-being.

Gratitude: Practicing gratitude can help shift our focus from negative emotions to positive ones. By recognizing the good in our lives, we can promote feelings of happiness and contentment.

Journaling: Writing down our thoughts and emotions can be a powerful tool for releasing negative energy. By putting our emotions on paper, we can gain clarity and perspective on the situation, and also work through our emotions in a healthy way.

Self-care: Taking care of ourselves physically, emotionally, and spiritually can also help release negative energy and promote emotional healing. This can include activities such as exercise, spending time in nature, or practicing self-compassion.

Overall, releasing negative energy and healing emotional wounds is a crucial part of the forgiveness process. By acknowledging our negative emotions, practicing forgiveness, and incorporating other healing practices into our daily lives, we can promote emotional healing, improve our relationships, and enhance our overall well-being.

Forgiving Yourself for Past Mistakes

Forgiving oneself is one of the most challenging tasks for many individuals, yet it is a critical step in the process of radical forgiveness. Self-forgiveness is the act of letting go of past mistakes, accepting oneself, and moving forward. It's important to understand that everyone makes mistakes, and it's natural to feel guilty or ashamed when we do. However, holding onto negative emotions and self-blame can cause significant emotional distress and hinder personal growth. In this chapter, we will explore the concept of self-forgiveness and the steps individuals can take to forgive themselves.

Acknowledge the Mistake

The first step towards self-forgiveness is acknowledging the mistake. It's essential to take responsibility for what we did, understand how it impacted others and ourselves, and take steps to rectify the situation if possible. Denying or avoiding the mistake can lead to further negative emotions and hinder the forgiveness process.

Accepting Imperfection

We all make mistakes; it's an inevitable part of being human. Accepting one, flaws and all, is an essential step in self-forgiveness. Individuals must acknowledge that perfection is unattainable, and making mistakes is a natural part of growth and learning. Accepting one self's imperfection is an act of self-compassion, which is essential in the forgiveness process.

Learning from the Mistake

Learning from past mistakes is an essential part of personal growth. Individuals must reflect on the mistake and understand what led them to act that way. This reflection helps individuals identify patterns in their behaviour and avoid repeating the same mistakes in the future. It's important to note that self-forgiveness doesn't mean forgetting the mistake entirely; it's about learning from the experience and moving forward.

Practice Self-Compassion

Practicing self-compassion is crucial in the forgiveness process. Individuals must understand that everyone makes mistakes and that negative self-talk and self-blame can hinder growth and healing. Practicing self-compassion involves treating oneself with the same kindness, concern, and care that we would offer a close friend or loved one. It's important to be gentle with oneself and offer words of encouragement during the forgiveness process.

Make Amends

Making amends is a vital step in the forgiveness process, especially when the mistake caused harm to others. Individuals must take responsibility for their actions, apologize sincerely, and take steps to make things right. Making amends shows a willingness to rectify the mistake and can help repair damaged relationships.

Letting Go

Letting go is the final step in the self-forgiveness process. It involves releasing negative emotions, such as guilt and shame, and moving forward. Letting go doesn't mean forgetting the mistake entirely, but rather accepting it as part of one's story and moving forward with newfound wisdom and growth. It's essential to remember that self-forgiveness is a process that takes time and effort, but the benefits of letting go of negative emotions are worth it.

Benefits of Self-Forgiveness

Practicing self-forgiveness can have a significant impact on mental health and well-being. Studies have shown that self-forgiveness is associated with lower levels of depression, anxiety, and stress. Additionally, individuals who practice self-forgiveness report higher levels of self-esteem, self-worth, and overall life satisfaction.

Self-forgiveness can also improve relationships with others. Individuals who practice self-forgiveness tend to be more empathetic and understanding towards others' mistakes and are more likely to offer forgiveness to those who have wronged them.

The Role of Compassion in Radical Forgiveness

Compassion is a critical component of radical forgiveness. When we are wronged or hurt by someone else, it can be easy to become angry, resentful, and bitter towards them. However, holding onto these negative emotions only serves to harm us and our relationships with others. Compassion, on the other hand, allows us to see the humanity in ourselves and others, and to let go of our grievances in a way that is both healing and transformative.

Compassion is defined as the ability to feel empathy and understanding towards others, even in difficult or painful situations. When we approach forgiveness from a place of compassion, we are able to recognize that everyone makes mistakes and has the potential for growth and change. We can see the other person as a whole, complex human being, with their own struggles, fears, and limitations. This understanding can help us let go of our anger and resentment, and replace it with a sense of empathy and kindness towards the other person.

In order to cultivate compassion in the forgiveness process, it is important to practice self-compassion first. This means recognizing our own mistakes and flaws, and treating ourselves with the same empathy and understanding that we hope to extend to others. When we are able to forgive ourselves, we are better equipped to forgive others as well.

Compassion also involves acknowledging the pain that we and others have experienced. When we hold onto anger and resentment, it can be easy to minimize or dismiss the harm that has been done. However, by acknowledging the pain, we can begin to process and heal from it. This doesn't mean we have to condone the actions of the person who hurt us, but rather, we can understand that they were likely acting from a place of pain or fear themselves.

In addition, cultivating compassion requires us to let go of the need for revenge or retribution. When we are hurt, our initial reaction may be to seek justice or vindication. However, this often perpetuates a cycle of harm, and prevents us from truly moving on. By letting go of the need for revenge, we open ourselves up to the possibility of healing and reconciliation.

One powerful way to cultivate compassion in the forgiveness process is through the practice of loving-kindness meditation. This practice involves silently repeating phrases of kindness and compassion towards ourselves and others. It can help us develop a sense of empathy and understanding towards those who have hurt us, and to extend forgiveness and compassion to ourselves as well.

In addition to loving-kindness meditation, other practices such as journaling, therapy, and mindful self-reflection can also be helpful in cultivating compassion in the forgiveness process. These practices can help us identify our own patterns of thought and behaviour, and can help us recognize the humanity and complexity of others.

Ultimately, compassion is a key component of radical forgiveness, and is essential for healing and transformation. By cultivating empathy and understanding towards ourselves and others, we can let go of our anger and resentment, and move towards a place of healing and growth.

The Importance of Forgiveness in Interpersonal Relationships

Interpersonal relationships can be challenging and complex, with many ups and downs. Misunderstandings, hurt feelings, and conflicts can arise, and if not handled properly, they can damage the relationship irreparably. One of the keys to maintaining healthy and fulfilling relationships is forgiveness. Forgiveness is essential for building trust, promoting emotional healing, and fostering empathy.

The Importance of Forgiveness in Interpersonal Relationships

Forgiveness is the act of letting go of anger, resentment, and the desire for revenge towards someone who has wronged us. In interpersonal relationships, forgiveness can be critical to restoring trust and repairing damaged relationships. When we forgive someone, we release ourselves from the burden of negative emotions, allowing us to move forward and heal emotionally.

Forgiveness promotes emotional healing by reducing feelings of anger, bitterness, and resentment. These negative emotions can lead to physical and psychological health problems, such as anxiety, depression, and even heart disease. When we forgive, we are able to let go of these negative emotions, allowing us to experience greater emotional well-being.

Forgiveness is also essential for building trust. When someone wrongs us, it can be difficult to trust them again.

However, if the person apologizes and takes responsibility for their actions, forgiveness can help us to rebuild trust. Forgiveness allows us to move beyond the hurt and betrayal, allowing us to focus on the present and future instead of dwelling on the past.

Forgiveness fosters empathy and understanding, allowing us to see things from another person's perspective. When we forgive someone, we are able to see beyond their actions and understand the circumstances that led them to act the way they did. This understanding can lead to greater empathy and compassion, allowing us to develop more meaningful and fulfilling relationships.

Forgiveness can also help us to avoid repeating negative patterns in our relationships. When we hold onto anger and resentment, we may unintentionally perpetuate negative behaviours that led to the conflict in the first place. Forgiveness allows us to break free from these patterns, promoting more positive interactions and behaviours in our relationships.

Practicing Forgiveness in Interpersonal Relationships

Forgiveness is a process that requires time and effort, but it is an essential part of maintaining healthy and fulfilling relationships. Here are some strategies for practicing forgiveness in interpersonal relationships:

Acknowledge your feelings: It's important to acknowledge your feelings and allow yourself to experience them fully. Denying or suppressing your feelings can lead to more negative emotions, such as anger and resentment.

Communicate with the other person: It's important to communicate with the other person about how their actions have affected you. Expressing your feelings in a calm and respectful manner can help the other person understand how their actions have hurt you and can open the door for a conversation about how to move forward?

Listen to the other person: It's important to listen to the other person's perspective and try to understand their point of view. This can help to promote empathy and compassion, allowing you to see things from their perspective.

Take responsibility for your own actions: It's important to take responsibility for your own actions and to acknowledge any part you may have played in the conflict. This can help to promote a sense of accountability and can help to avoid repeating negative patterns in the future.

Practice empathy and compassion: Practicing empathy and compassion can help to foster forgiveness and promote healing. Try to put yourself in the other person's shoes and understand the circumstances that led them to act the way they did.

Give yourself time: Forgiveness is a process that takes time, and it's important to be patient with yourself and with the other person. Allow yourself the time you need to heal emotionally and to work through any negative emotions you may be experiencing.

The Process of Reconciliation

The process of forgiveness is a journey that can lead to reconciliation, but it is important to understand that reconciliation is not the same as forgiveness. Forgiveness is a personal decision to let go of anger and resentment towards someone who has wronged us, while reconciliation involves restoring trust and rebuilding a relationship with the person who has hurt us.

Reconciliation is not always possible or even desirable, and it should only be attempted when both parties are willing to put in the effort to repair the relationship. However, if both parties are committed to the process, it can lead to a stronger and healthier relationship than before.

The first step in the process of reconciliation is communication. It is important to have an open and honest conversation with the person who has hurt you, expressing how you feel and listening to their perspective as well. This can be a difficult and emotional process, but it is essential for both parties to fully understand each other's thoughts and feelings.

Once both parties have expressed themselves and listened to each other, it is important to identify the root causes of the conflict. Often, conflicts arise from misunderstandings or unmet needs, and it is important to address these underlying issues to prevent similar conflicts from arising in the future.

The next step is to acknowledge the harm that was caused and to take responsibility for any actions that contributed to the conflict. This requires humility and a willingness to admit fault and ask for forgiveness.

If both parties are committed to the process of reconciliation, it is important to establish clear boundaries and expectations for the future. This may involve setting ground rules for communication and behaviour, as well as agreeing to seek outside help if needed.

Finally, it is important to work towards rebuilding trust and restoring the relationship. This can be a slow and difficult process, but it is essential for both parties to be patient and committed to the process.

In some cases, reconciliation may not be possible or may not be the best option. It is important to recognize when it is time to let go of a relationship and move on. However, even in these situations, forgiveness can still be a powerful tool for personal healing and growth.

In summary, the process of reconciliation requires open communication, a willingness to acknowledge and take responsibility for past actions, and a commitment to rebuilding trust and restoring the relationship. It can be a challenging journey, but if both parties are willing to put in the effort, it can lead to a stronger and healthier relationship than before.

The Power of Apology in the Forgiveness Process

The act of apologizing is a powerful tool in the process of forgiveness. When we acknowledge that we have caused harm to someone else and take responsibility for our actions, we create a pathway for healing and reconciliation. In this chapter, we will explore the power of apology in the forgiveness process, how to give a meaningful apology, and the benefits of offering and accepting apologies.

Why Apology Matters

Apologies play a crucial role in repairing relationships and rebuilding trust. When we hurt someone, we create a rift between us and the other person. An apology is a way of acknowledging that harm and demonstrating that we are willing to take responsibility for our actions. This can go a long way in repairing the relationship and restoring trust.

Apologies also have psychological benefits for both the person giving the apology and the person receiving it. For the person offering the apology, it can provide a sense of relief and release from guilt or shame. For the person receiving the apology, it can offer a sense of validation and acknowledgement that their feelings and experiences matter.

The Elements of a Meaningful Apology

A meaningful apology consists of several key elements. First, it should be sincere. A genuine apology involves taking responsibility for one's actions and expressing regret for the harm caused. It should not be done simply to appease the other person or to get them to forgive us.

Second, a meaningful apology should be specific. It should acknowledge the specific harm that was caused and the impact it had on the other person. This demonstrates that we have taken the time to understand their perspective and are truly sorry for what we have done.

Third, a meaningful apology should include a commitment to change. If we have caused harm, we need to take steps to ensure that we do not repeat the same behaviour in the future. This might involve making amends or changing our behaviour in some way.

Finally, a meaningful apology should be delivered in a timely manner. Waiting too long to apologize can make the other person feel like their feelings and experiences are not important to us. It is important to apologize as soon as possible after the harm has occurred.

Benefits of Offering and Accepting Apologies

Offering and accepting apologies can have numerous benefits for both the person giving the apology and the person receiving it. For the person offering the apology, it can provide a sense of relief and release from guilt or shame. It can also help to repair the relationship and restore trust.

For the person receiving the apology, it can offer a sense of validation and acknowledgement that their feelings and experiences matter. It can also help to heal emotional wounds and create a pathway for forgiveness.

In addition, research has shown that offering and accepting apologies can have physical and emotional health benefits. Apologizing has been linked to lower levels of stress and anxiety, improved sleep, and a greater sense of well-being. Accepting apologies has been linked to higher levels of forgiveness and greater relationship satisfaction.

Barriers to Apologizing

Despite the numerous benefits of offering and accepting apologies, there are often barriers that prevent people from apologizing. These barriers can include feelings of shame or embarrassment, fear of rejection, or a belief that apologizing is a sign of weakness.

It is important to recognize these barriers and work to overcome them in order to give and receive apologies effectively. This might involve practicing self-compassion and acknowledging that making mistakes is a normal part of being human. It might also involve learning effective communication skills and strategies for managing difficult emotions.

Conclusion

The act of apologizing is a powerful tool in the process of forgiveness. It allows us to take responsibility for our actions, acknowledge the harm we have caused, and demonstrate our commitment to change. By offering and accepting apologies, we can repair relationships, restore trust, and create a pathway for healing and reconciliation.

Forgiving Someone Who Has Hurt You Deeply

Forgiveness is an essential component of emotional healing and can be especially challenging when dealing with someone who has hurt us deeply. It may seem impossible to let go of the anger and resentment we hold towards this person. However, holding onto these negative emotions only leads to further pain and suffering. Forgiveness is a way to release these negative emotions and move towards healing and peace.

Here are some steps to take when seeking to forgive someone who has hurt you deeply:

Acknowledge the Pain

The first step towards forgiveness is to acknowledge the pain that you feel. It is important to allow yourself to experience the full range of emotions, including anger, sadness, and betrayal. Denying or suppressing these feelings will only prolong the healing process. Allow yourself to feel the pain, but do not get stuck in it.

Take Responsibility for Your Own Feelings

While the person who hurt you may have caused your pain, it is important to take responsibility for your own feelings. Recognize that your emotions are your own and that no one can make you feel a certain way. By taking responsibility for your own feelings, you empower yourself to change how you feel and respond to the situation.

Practice Empathy

Empathy is the ability to understand and share the feelings of another person. Try to put yourself in the shoes of the person who hurt you and imagine what they may have been going through at the time. This does not excuse their actions, but it can help you understand why they did what they did.

Let Go of Blame

Blaming the person who hurt you may feel satisfying in the moment, but it does not lead to healing or forgiveness. Blame keeps you stuck in the past and prevents you from moving forward. Let go of blame and focus on your own healing.

Practice Self-Compassion

Forgiving someone who has hurt you deeply can be challenging, and it is important to be kind to yourself during this process. Practice self-compassion by treating yourself with the same kindness and understanding that you would offer to a friend in a similar situation.

Consider the Benefits of Forgiveness

Forgiveness is a powerful tool for healing and can bring many benefits to your life. Research has shown that forgiveness can lead to reduced anxiety and depression, improved physical health, and stronger relationships. Consider the positive impact that forgiveness could have on your life.

Take Action

Forgiveness is not just a feeling, but also a decision and a process. Take action towards forgiveness by communicating with the person who hurt you, seeking professional help if necessary, and practicing self-care.

Be Patient

Forgiveness is a journey that takes time and patience. Do not expect to feel completely healed overnight. Be patient with yourself and trust the process of forgiveness.

In conclusion, forgiving someone who has hurt you deeply can be a difficult and challenging process, but it is also a powerful tool for healing and moving forward. By acknowledging the pain, taking responsibility for your own feelings, practicing empathy, letting go of blame, practicing self-compassion, considering the benefits of forgiveness, taking action, and being patient, you can begin to release the anger and resentment and move towards peace and healing.

Dealing with Abusive Relationships and Letting Go of Resentment

Abusive relationships can cause intense emotional pain and can be challenging to let go of resentment. It is common for people who have experienced abuse to struggle with feelings of anger, hurt, and betrayal long after the relationship has ended. However, holding onto these feelings can prevent healing and growth.

The first step in letting go of resentment towards an abusive partner is recognizing that the abuse was not your fault. Often, abusers manipulate and blame their victims for their behaviour, making them feel responsible for the abuse. However, it is essential to understand that no one deserves to be mistreated, and abuse is never justified.

The next step is to seek support. Talking to a therapist, support group, or trusted friend can help process emotions and provide a safe space to express feelings without judgment. It can also help to create a safety plan if the abuser tries to contact or harm you.

It is crucial to take time to heal and work on self-care. This can involve activities that bring joy, such as exercise, meditation, or creative outlets. It can also mean setting boundaries with people or situations that trigger negative emotions.

Forgiving an abusive partner does not mean forgetting what happened or excusing their behaviour. Instead, it is about releasing the hold that resentment has over your life and moving towards a future without bitterness. Forgiveness can lead to a sense of inner peace and can be a powerful tool in healing.

However, forgiveness should never be forced or rushed. It is a personal process and can take time. It is essential to prioritize your safety and well-being above all else and seek professional help if needed.

One technique for working towards forgiveness is to practice empathy. This involves trying to understand the abuser's perspective and recognizing the factors that led to their behaviour, such as past trauma or mental illness. It does not mean condoning their behaviour but can help develop compassion towards them as a person.

Another technique is to reframe the situation. Instead of focusing on the pain caused by the abuse, try to find meaning in the experience. For example, it may have led to personal growth, resilience, or empathy towards others who have experienced abuse.

In some cases, it may not be possible to forgive an abusive partner fully. However, working towards acceptance can be a step towards letting go of resentment. Acceptance involves acknowledging the reality of the situation and finding ways to move forward despite the pain.

In conclusion, letting go of resentment towards an abusive partner can be a challenging but necessary process for healing and growth. Seeking support, practicing self-care, and prioritizing safety are crucial steps in this journey. Forgiveness can be a powerful tool in this process, but it should never be forced or rushed. Instead, it is a personal process that takes time and can involve practicing empathy, reframing the situation, or working towards acceptance.

Letting Go of Anger towards Parents and Family Members

Family relationships can be some of the most complex and emotionally charged relationships in our lives. While we may feel a deep love and connection with our family members, we may also experience anger, frustration, and resentment towards them. This can be especially true when it comes to our parents and other close relatives.

Many of us carry emotional wounds and grievances from childhood that continue to affect us as adults. Whether it's a parent who was emotionally distant, abusive, or neglectful, or a sibling who was constantly critical, it's common to feel anger and resentment towards family members who hurt us in some way.

But holding on to this anger and resentment can be incredibly damaging, both to ourselves and to our relationships with our family members. It can lead to a cycle of bitterness and resentment that can be difficult to break, and can prevent us from building the kind of close and supportive relationships that we crave.

In this chapter, we will explore the process of letting go of anger towards parents and family members, and how forgiveness can help us heal and move forward.

Acknowledge the Pain

The first step in letting go of anger towards family members is to acknowledge the pain that you feel. It can be difficult to confront these emotions, especially if they have been buried for a long time, but it is important to allow yourself to feel and process the pain.

Take some time to reflect on your experiences with your family members. Think about the ways in which they have hurt you, and how this has affected your life. Allow yourself to feel the anger, sadness, and any other emotions that come up for you.

It's important to remember that acknowledging your pain does not mean that you are condoning or excusing your family members' behaviour. Rather, it is a way to give yourself permission to feel your emotions, and to begin the process of healing.

Practice Self-Compassion

Forgiveness starts with compassion, and this includes compassion for ourselves. It's important to recognize that the pain we feel is real, and that it is not our fault. We may have been victimized by our family members, but we are not defined by our victimhood.

Self-compassion involves treating ourselves with kindness, understanding, and acceptance. It means acknowledging our pain without judgment or self-blame, and offering ourselves the same kind of compassion and empathy that we would offer to a friend.

One way to practice self-compassion is to write a letter to yourself, acknowledging the pain that you feel and offering yourself words of kindness and support. This can be a powerful way to validate your emotions and start the process of healing.

Recognize Your Family Members' Humanity

It can be easy to see our family members as villains, especially if they have hurt us deeply. But it's important to remember that they are human beings, with their own flaws, struggles, and pain.

When we recognize our family members' humanity, we are more able to understand their actions and see them in a more compassionate light. This doesn't mean that we have to condone or excuse their behaviour, but it can help us to let go of our anger and resentment towards them.

One way to cultivate compassion towards our family members is to try to see the world from their perspective. What challenges have they faced in their lives? What might have led them to act the way that they did? This exercise can help us to develop empathy towards our family members, and to let go of the anger and resentment that we feel towards them.

Practice Forgiveness

Forgiveness is a process, not a one-time event. It involves acknowledging our pain, practicing self-compassion, and cultivating compassion towards the person who hurt us. It also involves making a conscious decision to let go of our anger and resentment, and to release ourselves from the burden of these emotions.

The journey of forgiveness can be a challenging process, especially when you have experienced trauma. Trauma can come in different forms such as physical, emotional, and psychological, and can be caused by different events, such as abuse, violence, and natural disasters. Trauma can leave a lasting impact on a person's life, leading to feelings of anger, fear, and resentment.

Forgiving the unforgivable can feel impossible, especially when the person who caused the trauma shows no remorse. However, forgiveness is not about condoning the actions of the offender or forgetting what happened, but rather, it's about finding a way to move forward and find peace in your life.

The first step towards forgiveness is acknowledging and accepting the trauma that you have experienced. It's important to understand that trauma can impact different people in different ways, and there is no right or wrong way to react. You may experience a range of emotions, including anger, sadness, and fear, and it's important to allow yourself to feel and process these emotions.

The next step is to confront the person who caused the trauma, but only if it's safe to do so. Confrontation can help you gain closure and communicate the impact of their actions on your life. However, it's important to approach the situation with a clear mind and to avoid blaming or attacking the person. Instead, focus on expressing how their actions affected you and your life.

If it's not safe or possible to confront the person, you can still find ways to release your anger and resentment. One approach is to write a letter to the person, expressing your feelings and thoughts. You don't have to send the letter, but writing it down can help you process your emotions and gain some closure.

Another approach is to seek therapy or support from a trusted friend or family member. Trauma can leave a lasting impact on a person's mental health, and seeking professional help can provide you with tools to process your emotions and find a way forward.

It's important to understand that forgiveness is a process and it takes time. You may need to revisit the trauma multiple times, and each time you do, you may experience a different set of emotions. Forgiveness is not a linear process, and it's important to be patient and kind to yourself as you work through it.

Forgiveness is not about forgetting what happened, but rather, it's about finding a way to live with the trauma and move forward. It's important to focus on your own healing and not allow the trauma to define your life. You can find ways to take control of your life and find happiness, even in the face of adversity.

In conclusion, forgiving the unforgivable is a difficult process, especially when you have experienced trauma. It's important to acknowledge and accept your emotions, confront the person if it's safe to do so, and seek support from trusted sources. Forgiveness is a process, and it's Important to be patient and kind to yourself as you work through it. Remember, forgiveness is not about forgetting what happened, but rather, finding a way to live with the trauma and move forward.

The Connection between Forgiveness and Gratitude

Gratitude and forgiveness are two powerful emotions that can greatly impact our lives. While they may seem like unrelated emotions, they are actually closely connected. In fact, practicing gratitude can enhance our ability to forgive, and forgiving can increase our capacity for gratitude.

Gratitude is the feeling of appreciation for the things and people in our lives. It is the recognition of the good things that we have received, and it involves acknowledging the role of others in bringing those good things into our lives. Gratitude has been linked to numerous benefits, including increased happiness, better relationships, improved physical health, and reduced stress.

Forgiveness, on the other hand, is the act of letting go of resentment, anger, and the desire for revenge towards someone who has wronged us. It is a complex process that involves acknowledging the harm that has been done, choosing to release negative emotions, and finding a way to move forward. Forgiveness has been shown to have numerous benefits as well, including reduced stress, improved mental health, better physical health, and stronger relationships.

So, how are gratitude and forgiveness connected? First, gratitude can help us to see the positive aspects of the situation and the person who has wronged us. It can help us to focus on the good that we have received from that person, even if it is overshadowed by the harm. By recognizing the good, we can develop a more balanced perspective on the situation, which can help us to be more open to forgiveness.

Gratitude can also help us to feel more empathy and compassion towards the person who has wronged us. When we focus on the good things that they have done for us, it can help us to see them as complex human beings with both good and bad qualities. This can help us to understand their actions in a more nuanced way and can make it easier to forgive them.

Forgiveness, in turn, can increase our capacity for gratitude. When we forgive someone, we are choosing to let go of negative emotions and focus on positive ones. This can open up space for gratitude to emerge. By releasing anger and resentment, we can start to see the good that exists in our lives and appreciate it more fully.

Forgiveness can also help us to deepen our relationships with others. When we forgive someone, we are showing them that we are willing to work through difficulties and that we value our relationship with them. This can create a sense of gratitude for the people in our lives who are willing to work through problems with us.

So, how can we cultivate both gratitude and forgiveness in our lives? Here are some strategies:

Practice gratitude regularly. Take time each day to think about the good things in your life and express appreciation for them. This can help to shift your focus towards the positive aspects of your life and make it easier to forgive.

Practice forgiveness regularly. Look for opportunities to forgive others, even for minor transgressions. This can help you to develop the habit of forgiveness and make it easier to forgive in more challenging situations.

Recognize the humanity of others. Try to see others as complex human beings with both good and bad qualities. This can help you to develop empathy and compassion, which can make forgiveness easier.

Communicate your gratitude and forgiveness to others. Let the people in your life know that you appreciate them and are willing to forgive them. This can create a sense of connection and deepen your relationships.

Take care of yourself. Practicing gratitude and forgiveness can be emotionally challenging. Make sure to take care of yourself by getting enough rest, eating well, and engaging in activities that bring you joy.

Forgiving Those Who Have Passed Away

Losing someone you love is one of the most difficult experiences that one can go through in life. The pain of grief can be overwhelming, and it can be challenging to find peace when you are consumed by feelings of anger, resentment, and even guilt towards the person who has passed away. However, it is important to understand that holding onto these negative emotions can hinder your healing process and prevent you from finding closure.

Forgiving someone who has passed away may seem like an impossible task, but it is a necessary step towards healing and finding peace. Forgiveness is not about forgetting what has happened or excusing the actions of the person who has passed away. Instead, it is about acknowledging the pain and hurt that they may have caused you and finding a way to let go of the negative emotions that are holding you back.

One way to begin the forgiveness process is by writing a letter to the person who has passed away. This letter is not intended to be sent or even read by anyone else; it is simply a way for you to express your feelings and thoughts to the person who has passed away. Write about your pain, your anger, your disappointment, and anything else that you are feeling. Once you have finished writing, read the letter out loud, and allow yourself to feel the emotions that come up. This exercise can be cathartic and help you release some of the negative energy that you are holding onto.

Another strategy is to focus on the positive memories that you have of the person who has passed away. Reflect on the moments of joy, love, and happiness that you shared with them. These memories can help shift your focus from the negative emotions to the positive ones, and help you find a sense of peace and closure.

Additionally, practicing self-compassion and self-forgiveness is crucial when dealing with the loss of a loved one. Acknowledge that you are human, and it is natural to experience a wide range of emotions after losing someone you love. Be kind to yourself and allow yourself to grieve at your own pace.

It is also essential to seek support from others during the grieving process. Talk to a trusted friend or family member, join a support group, or seek the help of a professional therapist. These resources can provide you with a safe space to express your feelings and thoughts and offer guidance on how to move forward.

In conclusion, forgiving someone who has passed away can be a challenging and emotional process, but it is an essential step towards finding peace and closure. By acknowledging your pain, focusing on positive memories, practicing self-compassion, and seeking support from others, you can find a way to let go of the negative emotions and move towards healing. Remember that forgiveness is not about forgetting, but rather about finding a way to release the pain and hurt that is holding you back from finding peace.

Overcoming Workplace Conflict through Forgiveness

Workplace conflict is a common occurrence that can lead to stress, anxiety, and decreased productivity. Conflict can arise from differences in opinion, communication breakdowns, competition, and power struggles. Forgiveness is a powerful tool for overcoming workplace conflict and improving relationships between colleagues. In this chapter, we will explore the role of forgiveness in resolving workplace conflict and provide strategies for practicing forgiveness in the workplace.

The Benefits of Forgiveness in the Workplace

Forgiveness has numerous benefits in the workplace. When employees practice forgiveness, they are more likely to experience positive emotions, such as happiness and satisfaction. They are also more likely to have better relationships with their colleagues, leading to increased collaboration and teamwork.

Forgiveness can also reduce stress and anxiety, which can improve overall job satisfaction and productivity. When employees hold onto grudges and negative feelings towards colleagues, they may become distracted and less engaged in their work, leading to decreased performance.

Additionally, practicing forgiveness can lead to a more positive workplace culture. When employees forgive one another, they create a more compassionate and supportive environment, which can lead to increased motivation and job satisfaction.

Strategies for Practicing Forgiveness in the Workplace

Communicate openly and honestly: Misunderstandings and communication breakdowns can often lead to workplace conflict. By communicating openly and honestly with colleagues, employees can address issues before they escalate into larger conflicts.

Take responsibility for your own actions: When conflict arises, it's important to take responsibility for your own actions and apologize if necessary. This can help defuse the situation and show colleagues that you are committed to resolving the conflict.

Try to see the situation from the other person's perspective: Empathy is a key component of forgiveness. By trying to see the situation from the other person's perspective, employees can gain a better understanding of the root of the conflict and work towards a resolution.

Focus on the present moment: It's important to let go of past grievances and focus on the present moment. Dwelling on past conflicts can prevent employees from moving forward and finding a solution to the current issue.

Practice active listening: Active listening involves fully engaging in a conversation and giving the speaker your full attention. By practicing active listening, employees can demonstrate empathy and gain a better understanding of their colleague's perspective.

Seek the help of a mediator: In some cases, it may be necessary to seek the help of a mediator to resolve workplace conflict. A mediator can help facilitate a conversation between colleagues and work towards a resolution that is satisfactory for both parties.

Conclusion

Forgiveness is a powerful tool for overcoming workplace conflict and improving relationships between colleagues. By practicing forgiveness in the workplace, employees can experience numerous benefits, including increased job satisfaction, better relationships with colleagues, and a more positive workplace culture. By communicating openly and honestly, taking responsibility for their own actions, and practicing empathy, employees can work towards resolving workplace conflict and creating a more harmonious work environment.

The Role of Forgiveness in Addiction Recovery

Addiction recovery can be a challenging and complex process, and forgiveness can play an important role in helping individuals move forward and find healing. Addiction can cause a lot of pain, not just for the person struggling with it, but also for those around them. Addicts often hurt their loved ones, damage relationships, and may have engaged in dishonest or even illegal behaviour. In order to make progress in recovery, it is important to address these past hurts and take steps to repair relationships.

One of the keys to addiction recovery is addressing the underlying emotional pain and trauma that often drives addictive behaviours. This can involve confronting difficult emotions and memories, and working through the pain and shame that may have led to the addiction in the first place. Forgiveness can be an important tool in this process, as it allows individuals to let go of anger and resentment and move towards a place of healing.

Forgiveness is not about excusing or condoning harmful behaviour, but rather about releasing negative emotions and allowing oneself to move forward. This can be a difficult process, especially when it comes to forgiving oneself or forgiving those who have hurt us deeply. However, by practicing forgiveness, individuals can find a sense of peace and freedom from the emotional pain that often accompanies addiction.

In addiction recovery, forgiveness can take many forms. It may involve forgiving oneself for past mistakes and harm caused to others, as well as forgiving those who may have contributed to one's addiction, such as family members or friends who enabled or ignored the problem. It may also involve seeking forgiveness from those who have been hurt, and making amends to repair damaged relationships.

Forgiveness can be a powerful tool in addiction recovery, but it is important to recognize that it is not a one-time event. Rather, it is a process that takes time and effort, and may involve setbacks and struggles along the way. However, by practicing forgiveness and focusing on healing and growth, individuals can find a renewed sense of purpose and hope in their recovery journey.

One way to cultivate forgiveness in addiction recovery is through mindfulness and self-compassion practices. These practices can help individuals to become more aware of their thoughts and emotions, and to develop a greater sense of self-acceptance and compassion. By cultivating a sense of self-compassion and forgiveness, individuals can begin to let go of negative self-talk and self-blame, and move towards a more positive and healing mind-set.

Another important aspect of forgiveness in addiction recovery is seeking support and guidance from others. This may involve working with a therapist or counsellor, joining a support group, or seeking guidance from a spiritual or religious leader. By sharing their struggles and experiences with others, individuals can gain valuable insights and perspective, and find the support they need to move forward in their recovery journey.

In conclusion, forgiveness can play an important role in addiction recovery, helping individuals to let go of negative emotions and move towards healing and growth. Whether it involves forgiving oneself, seeking forgiveness from others, or letting go of resentment towards those who have contributed to one's addiction, forgiveness is a powerful tool for building resilience and finding peace in the midst of difficulty. By cultivating forgiveness and focusing on growth and healing, individuals can overcome addiction and move towards a brighter future.

The Connection between Forgiveness and Physical Health

Forgiveness has long been associated with mental and emotional health, but research also suggests that there is a link between forgiveness and physical health. Holding onto anger, resentment, and grudges can have negative impacts on our bodies, leading to a variety of health problems. On the other hand, practicing forgiveness can have significant benefits for our physical health.

One way that forgiveness can improve physical health is by reducing stress. When we hold onto anger and resentment, our bodies release stress hormones such as cortisol and adrenaline. These hormones can have damaging effects on the body over time, leading to issues such as high blood pressure, heart disease, and weakened immune function. By practicing forgiveness, we can reduce the stress and negative emotions that lead to the release of these hormones.

Forgiveness can also have a positive impact on the cardiovascular system. Studies have found that people who practice forgiveness have lower blood pressure and a reduced risk of heart disease. Forgiveness may also help to reduce inflammation in the body, which is associated with a range of health problems including arthritis, asthma, and even cancer.

In addition to its effects on stress and physical health, forgiveness can also have indirect benefits for our bodies. When we hold onto anger and resentment, we may be more likely to engage in unhealthy behaviours such as overeating, substance abuse, and neglecting exercise. By practicing forgiveness, we may be more likely to engage in healthier behaviours that promote physical health.

One study found that participants who practiced forgiveness had lower levels of pain, better sleep quality, and improved physical functioning compared to those who did not practice forgiveness. Another study found that forgiveness was associated with a reduced risk of chronic illness and increased longevity.

It's important to note that forgiveness is not a magic cure-all for physical health problems. However, it can be a powerful tool for improving overall well-being and preventing the negative health effects of holding onto anger and resentment.

So how can we cultivate forgiveness for the sake of our physical health? Here are some strategies:

Practice mindfulness. Mindfulness meditation can help us to become more aware of our emotions and to cultivate compassion and understanding for ourselves and others.

Challenge negative thoughts. When negative thoughts about a person or situation arise, try to challenge them and reframe the situation in a more positive light.

Seek support. Forgiveness can be a difficult process, and it can be helpful to seek support from a therapist or trusted friend or family member.

Let go of control. Recognize that you cannot control the actions of others, but you can control your own thoughts and reactions. Focus on what you can control and let go of the rest.

Practice self-care. Take care of yourself physically and emotionally by engaging in healthy habits such as exercise, eating a nutritious diet, getting enough sleep, and engaging in activities that bring you joy.

In conclusion, forgiveness is not only beneficial for our mental and emotional well-being, but it also has important implications for our physical health. By practicing forgiveness, we can reduce stress, improve cardiovascular health, and engage in healthier behaviours overall. Cultivating forgiveness may not always be easy, but it is a powerful tool for promoting overall health and well-being.

Finding Forgiveness in Difficult Circumstances

Forgiveness is not always easy. In fact, sometimes it can be incredibly difficult to forgive someone who has wronged us. In some cases, the circumstances may be particularly challenging, such as when the harm caused is severe or when the person who has caused the harm is someone we care deeply about. In these situations, it may feel impossible to let go of anger and resentment and to find forgiveness.

However, even in the most difficult circumstances, forgiveness is possible. It may require more time, effort, and support, but with dedication and perseverance, it is possible to find forgiveness and move forward in a healthy way. Here are some strategies for finding forgiveness in difficult circumstances:

Seek support

If you are struggling to forgive someone, it can be helpful to seek support from others. This may include talking to a trusted friend, family member, or therapist. Having someone to listen to your thoughts and feelings can help you process your emotions and gain a new perspective on the situation. They may also be able to offer guidance and support as you work towards forgiveness.

Practice self-care

Taking care of yourself is essential when trying to find forgiveness in difficult circumstances. This may include engaging in activities that bring you joy, such as exercising, reading, or spending time with loved ones. It may also include practicing relaxation techniques, such as meditation or deep breathing exercises, to help reduce stress and promote feelings of calm.

Challenge negative thoughts

When we are struggling to forgive, it can be easy to get caught up in negative thoughts and emotions. However, it is important to challenge these thoughts and try to see the situation from a different perspective. Ask yourself questions such as, "What would I say to a friend who was in this situation?" or "Is there another way to look at this situation?" By challenging negative thoughts and looking for different perspectives, you may be able to find forgiveness more easily.

Set boundaries

In some cases, it may be necessary to set boundaries with the person who has caused harm in order to protect yourself and your well-being. This may include limiting contact, setting clear expectations for behaviour, or ending the relationship altogether. Setting boundaries can be a difficult but necessary step towards finding forgiveness.

Practice empathy

Empathy involves trying to understand the thoughts and feelings of another person. When trying to find forgiveness, practicing empathy can be incredibly helpful. Try to put yourself in the other person's shoes and imagine what they may have been going through at the time of the harm. This can help you gain a better understanding of their perspective and may make it easier to find forgiveness.

Focus on the future

Finally, it can be helpful to focus on the future when trying to find forgiveness in difficult circumstances. Instead of dwelling on the past and the harm that has been caused, focus on what you can do to move forward in a healthy way. This may involve setting goals, making plans for the future, and focusing on positive changes you can make in your life.

In conclusion, finding forgiveness in difficult circumstances is possible, but it may require more effort and support than in other situations. By seeking support, practicing self-care, challenging negative thoughts, setting boundaries, practicing empathy, and focusing on the future, you can work towards finding forgiveness and moving forward in a healthy way. Remember, forgiveness is a process, and it may take time, but with dedication and perseverance, it is possible.

Overcoming the Fear of Forgiveness

Forgiveness is a powerful tool that can help you heal emotional wounds, let go of anger and resentment, and move forward in your life. However, for some people, the idea of forgiveness can be scary and overwhelming. They may feel that forgiving someone means that they are condoning their behaviour or that they are letting the person off the hook for their actions. In this chapter, we will explore the fear of forgiveness and provide strategies for overcoming it.

Understanding the Fear of Forgiveness

The fear of forgiveness often stems from a misconception about what forgiveness is and what it means. Many people believe that forgiving someone means that they are saying that what the person did was okay, and this can feel like a betrayal of their own values and beliefs. However, this is not the case. Forgiveness is not about condoning bad behaviour or excusing it, but rather it is about releasing yourself from the negative emotions and thoughts that are holding you back.

Another reason that people may fear forgiveness is that it requires vulnerability. When you forgive someone, you are opening yourself up to the possibility of being hurt again. This can be scary, especially if the person who hurt you is someone you love and trust. However, it is important to remember that forgiveness is not about forgetting what happened or trusting the person again, but rather it is about letting go of the negative emotions and thoughts that are keeping you stuck.

Strategies for Overcoming the Fear of Forgiveness

Educate Yourself about Forgiveness

One of the best ways to overcome the fear of forgiveness is to educate yourself about what forgiveness is and what it is not. Read books, articles, and blog posts about forgiveness and try to understand the benefits that come with it. Talk to people who have forgiven others and ask them about their experiences. The more you know about forgiveness, the less scary it will seem.

Practice Self-Compassion

Forgiving someone can be difficult, especially if the hurt they caused was significant. Practice self-compassion by acknowledging the pain you feel and giving yourself permission to feel it. It is okay to take time to heal and work through your emotions. Be gentle with yourself and remember that forgiveness is a process.

Seek Support

If you are struggling with the fear of forgiveness, it can be helpful to seek support from a trusted friend, family member, or therapist. Talking about your feelings can help you process them and gain a new perspective. A therapist can also provide guidance and support as you work through the forgiveness process.

Start Small

Forgiveness can be a daunting task, especially if you are trying to forgive someone who has caused you significant harm. Start small by practicing forgiveness in smaller situations. For example, forgive someone who cut you off in traffic or forgive a friend who forgot your birthday. This can help you build the skills and confidence you need to tackle bigger forgiveness challenges.

Focus on the Benefits

When you are struggling with the fear of forgiveness, it can be helpful to focus on the benefits that come with forgiveness. Forgiveness can help you let go of anger and resentment, reduce stress and anxiety, and improve your relationships. Remembering these benefits can help motivate you to work through the fear and move towards forgiveness.

In conclusion, the fear of forgiveness can be a significant barrier to healing emotional wounds and moving forward in your life. However, with education, self-compassion, support, and practice, it is possible to overcome this fear and experience the many benefits that forgiveness has to offer. Remember that forgiveness is a process, and it is okay to take your time and work through it at your own pace. With patience and persistence, you can find peace and healing through forgiveness.

Healing the Inner Child through Forgiveness

The inner child refers to the vulnerable and innocent part of ourselves that experienced pain, trauma, and neglect during our childhood. These experiences can lead to deep emotional wounds that continue to affect our adult lives, causing us to struggle with low self-esteem, fear, anxiety, and negative patterns of behaviour.

Forgiveness is a powerful tool for healing these wounds and releasing the pain and anger that we hold towards ourselves and others. When we forgive, we let go of the resentment and hurt that keeps us stuck in the past and prevents us from moving forward.

In this chapter, we will explore how forgiveness can help heal the inner child and how to practice forgiveness for ourselves and others.

Understanding the Inner Child

The inner child is the part of us that is most vulnerable and sensitive to the world around us. When we experience trauma, neglect, or abuse, our inner child may become wounded, leading to feelings of abandonment, shame, and fear.

These feelings can stay with us into adulthood, causing us to struggle with relationships, self-esteem, and self-worth. We may develop negative patterns of behaviour and coping mechanisms to protect ourselves from the pain we experienced as children.

The inner child is a powerful force that can help us connect with our emotions, intuition, and creativity. When we are in touch with our inner child, we can access a deep well of wisdom and joy that can help us heal and grow.

Forgiving Ourselves and Others

Forgiveness is a crucial part of healing the inner child. When we forgive ourselves and others for past mistakes and pain, we release the negative emotions that keep us stuck in the past.

Forgiveness does not mean that we condone harmful behaviour or forget what happened. Instead, it means that we choose to let go of the anger and resentment that we hold towards ourselves and others.

Forgiveness is a choice, and it requires a willingness to let go of the past and move forward with compassion and understanding. We can practice forgiveness by:

Acknowledging our pain and the pain of others

Taking responsibility for our actions and the actions of others

Choosing to let go of the anger and resentment we hold towards ourselves and others

Focusing on compassion, empathy, and understanding

Practicing self-care and self-compassion

Healing the Inner Child through Forgiveness

Healing the inner child through forgiveness involves acknowledging and healing the emotional wounds we experienced as children. This process can be challenging, but it is essential for our emotional and mental health.

Here are some steps we can take to heal our inner child through forgiveness:

Identify the emotional wounds: The first step in healing the inner child is identifying the emotional wounds we experienced as children. We can do this by exploring our memories and feelings and acknowledging the pain we experienced.

Practice self-compassion: Self-compassion is a vital part of healing the inner child. We can practice self-compassion by treating ourselves with kindness, understanding, and forgiveness.

Practice forgiveness: Forgiveness is essential for healing the inner child. We can practice forgiveness by acknowledging the pain and suffering we experienced as children and choosing to let go of the anger and resentment we hold towards ourselves and others.

Connect with our inner child: Connecting with our inner child can help us access the wisdom, creativity, and joy that we experienced as children. We can connect with our inner child by engaging in activities that bring us joy, such as dancing, playing, or creating art.

Seek professional help: Healing the inner child can be a challenging process, and seeking professional help can be beneficial. A therapist or counsellor can help us identify and heal emotional wounds, develop healthy coping mechanisms, and practice forgiveness.

The Connection between Forgiveness and Happiness

Forgiveness and happiness are two concepts that are deeply intertwined. Forgiveness can be a powerful tool in promoting happiness and well-being, both in ourselves and in our relationships with others. In this chapter, we will explore the connection between forgiveness and happiness, and how forgiveness can help us to live a more joyful and fulfilling life.

When we hold onto anger, resentment, and bitterness towards others, it can weigh heavily on our hearts and minds. These negative emotions can consume us, making it difficult to find happiness and peace. By learning to forgive, we can release these negative emotions and find greater happiness and joy in our lives.

Research has shown that forgiveness can have a positive impact on both our mental and physical health. Forgiveness can reduce stress, anxiety, and depression, and increase feelings of happiness, contentment, and well-being. Forgiveness has also been linked to better physical health, including lower blood pressure and a reduced risk of heart disease.

One reason forgiveness may be so powerful in promoting happiness is that it allows us to let go of the past and live in the present. When we hold onto anger and resentment towards someone who has wronged us, we are living in the past, reliving the hurt and pain over and over again. By learning to forgive, we can release these negative emotions and focus on the present moment. This can help us to feel more present and engaged in our lives, and to find greater joy and happiness in the little things.

Another reason that forgiveness can be so powerful in promoting happiness is that it can improve our relationships with others. When we forgive someone, we are opening ourselves up to the possibility of deeper connection and understanding with that person. We are also creating space for greater love, kindness, and compassion in our lives. This can lead to more fulfilling relationships with others, and ultimately to greater happiness and well-being.

Learning to forgive is not always easy, especially when we have been deeply hurt by someone. It can take time, patience, and a willingness to let go of our anger and bitterness. However, the benefits of forgiveness are undeniable. By releasing our negative emotions and focusing on the present moment, we can find greater happiness and joy in our lives. By improving our relationships with others through forgiveness, we can create a more loving, kind, and compassionate world.

In conclusion, forgiveness and happiness are deeply interconnected. By learning to forgive, we can release our negative emotions and find greater happiness and joy in our lives. Forgiveness can also improve our relationships with others, leading to more fulfilling connections and ultimately to greater happiness and well-being. While forgiveness may not always be easy, the benefits are undeniable. By opening ourselves up to forgiveness, we can create a more peaceful, loving, and joyful world.

How to Avoid Future Resentment

Resentment is an unpleasant emotion that can take hold of us when we feel wronged or hurt by someone else's actions. While it is normal to feel this way, holding onto resentment can have negative consequences on our mental and emotional health. That's why it's important to learn how to avoid future resentment. In this chapter, we will explore some practical tips on how to do just that.

Practice Effective Communication

One of the most common reasons for resentment is a lack of effective communication. When we don't communicate our needs, feelings, or concerns, we are more likely to feel unheard or ignored. Over time, these feelings can turn into resentment. To avoid this, practice effective communication. Be clear and concise in expressing yourself, and listen actively to what others have to say. This can help to prevent misunderstandings and ensure that everyone is on the same page.

Set Clear Boundaries

Another common cause of resentment is when people overstep our boundaries. This could be in the form of someone repeatedly taking advantage of us, making unreasonable demands, or not respecting our time or space. To avoid future resentment, it's important to set clear boundaries. Be assertive in communicating what you are and are not comfortable with, and stick to these boundaries. This can help to prevent others from overstepping and causing you to feel resentful.

Practice Forgiveness

While forgiveness may seem counterintuitive to avoiding resentment, it can actually be a powerful tool in preventing it from taking hold. When we hold onto grudges or refuse to forgive others, we are more likely to feel bitter and resentful. On the other hand, practicing forgiveness can help to let go of negative emotions and prevent them from festering into resentment. It's important to note that forgiveness doesn't mean you have to forget or condone the other person's actions. Rather, it means letting go of the negative emotions associated with the situation and moving forward.

Practice Self-Care

Taking care of yourself is an essential part of avoiding future resentment. When we neglect our own needs or put others before ourselves, we can begin to feel resentful. To avoid this, make self-care a priority. Take time to do things you enjoy, prioritize rest and relaxation, and be mindful of your own needs. When you take care of yourself, you are better equipped to handle challenging situations without feeling resentful.

Practice Gratitude

Practicing gratitude is another powerful tool in avoiding future resentment. When we focus on the things we are grateful for, it can help to shift our perspective and prevent negative emotions from taking hold. Make a habit of reflecting on the things you are grateful for each day, no matter how small they may seem. This can help to cultivate a more positive outlook and prevent resentment from taking root.

In conclusion, avoiding future resentment requires a combination of effective communication, boundary setting, forgiveness, self-care, and gratitude. By practicing these habits, you can create a more positive and fulfilling life that is free from the burden of resentment. Remember, letting go of resentment isn't always easy, but it's worth it for the peace and happiness it can bring into your life.

The Connection between Forgiveness and Emotional Intelligence

Emotional intelligence is the ability to identify, understand, and manage one's emotions and the emotions of others. It is an important skill for individuals to develop because it can have a significant impact on personal and professional success. Emotional intelligence can also play a key role in the forgiveness process. In this chapter, we will explore the connection between forgiveness and emotional intelligence.

Emotional intelligence is made up of several components, including self-awareness, self-regulation, motivation, empathy, and social skills. These components are closely related to the forgiveness process. For example, self-awareness is important because it helps individuals identify their emotions and understand why they are feeling a certain way. This is essential for forgiveness because it allows individuals to recognize when they are feeling resentful or angry towards someone and take steps to address those feelings.

Self-regulation is another important component of emotional intelligence that is closely related to forgiveness. Self-regulation refers to an individual's ability to control their emotions and behaviours. This is important in the forgiveness process because it allows individuals to manage their feelings of anger or resentment and choose a more forgiving response.

Motivation is also an important component of emotional intelligence. Motivation refers to an individual's drive to achieve their goals. In the context of forgiveness, motivation can be important because it can help individuals stay committed to the forgiveness process even when it is difficult.

Empathy is another important component of emotional intelligence that is closely related to forgiveness. Empathy refers to an individual's ability to understand and share the feelings of others. This is important in the forgiveness process because it allows individuals to understand the perspective of the person who has hurt them and see things from their point of view.

Finally, social skills are an important component of emotional intelligence. Social skills refer to an individual's ability to communicate effectively with others and build positive relationships. This is important in the forgiveness process because it allows individuals to communicate their feelings effectively and work towards repairing damaged relationships.

In order to develop emotional intelligence in the context of forgiveness, there are several steps individuals can take. First, individuals can work on developing self-awareness by practicing mindfulness and reflecting on their emotions. This can help individuals recognize when they are feeling angry or resentful towards someone and take steps to address those feelings.

Second, individuals can work on developing self-regulation by practicing relaxation techniques such as deep breathing or meditation. This can help individuals manage their emotions and respond to difficult situations in a more forgiving way.

Third, individuals can work on developing empathy by practicing active listening and trying to understand the perspective of the person who has hurt them. This can help individuals see things from a different point of view and understand why the person may have acted in a certain way.

Fourth, individuals can work on developing social skills by practicing effective communication and conflict resolution skills. This can help individuals communicate their feelings effectively and work towards repairing damaged relationships.

In conclusion, emotional intelligence is an important component of the forgiveness process. By developing skills such as self-awareness, self-regulation, motivation, empathy, and social skills, individuals can improve their ability to forgive others and let go of resentment. By practicing these skills, individuals can also improve their personal and professional relationships and achieve greater success in all areas of their lives.

Forgiveness and the Power of Positive Thinking

Forgiveness is not an easy task, but it is a crucial component of leading a positive and fulfilling life. When we hold onto grudges and resentments, we trap ourselves in negativity and prevent ourselves from moving forward. Instead of focusing on what we cannot change, we can choose to forgive and free ourselves from the burden of negative emotions.

One powerful tool in cultivating forgiveness is the power of positive thinking. Positive thinking is the practice of focusing on the positive aspects of our lives, rather than dwelling on the negative. When we focus on the positive, we are more likely to experience positive outcomes and emotions.

Here are some ways in which positive thinking can help us in the forgiveness process:

Seeing the good in others: Positive thinking can help us see the good in others, even when they have wronged us. Instead of dwelling on their negative actions, we can focus on their positive qualities and intentions. This shift in perspective can make it easier for us to forgive and move forward.

Cultivating empathy: Positive thinking can also help us cultivate empathy for those who have hurt us. When we focus on the positive aspects of their lives, we can better understand their perspective and motivations. This can help us see them as flawed human beings, rather than as villains who intentionally hurt us.

Letting go of negative emotions: Positive thinking can help us let go of negative emotions, such as anger, resentment, and bitterness. When we focus on positive thoughts and emotions, we create a shift in our brain chemistry that allows us to let go of negative emotions more easily.

Attracting positive experiences: Finally, positive thinking can help us attract positive experiences into our lives. When we focus on positive thoughts and emotions, we are more likely to experience positive outcomes in our relationships, career, and personal life.

Of course, positive thinking alone is not enough to cultivate forgiveness. We must also be willing to do the hard work of processing our emotions, practicing empathy, and communicating our needs and boundaries. However, by adopting a positive mind-set, we can create a foundation of positivity and hope that can help us navigate the forgiveness process more easily.

In order to cultivate positive thinking, there are several techniques that we can use:

Gratitude: Practicing gratitude is a powerful way to focus on the positive aspects of our lives. By taking time each day to reflect on what we are thankful for, we can shift our focus away from negative thoughts and emotions.

Affirmations: Affirmations are positive statements that we can repeat to ourselves throughout the day. By affirming positive beliefs about ourselves and our lives, we can create a positive mind-set that can help us forgive more easily.

Visualization: Visualization is the practice of imagining positive outcomes and experiences. By visualizing positive scenarios in our minds, we can create a sense of hope and possibility that can help us move forward.

Mindfulness: Mindfulness is the practice of being present in the moment and focusing on our thoughts and emotions without judgment. By practicing mindfulness, we can become more aware of our negative thought patterns and replace them with positive ones.

In conclusion, forgiveness is a powerful tool for creating positive change in our lives. By adopting a positive mind-set, we can cultivate the empathy, gratitude, and hope that we need to move forward and let go of negative emotions. While forgiveness is not always easy, the benefits of forgiveness are clear: increased happiness, inner peace, and improved relationships with others. With practice and patience, we can all learn to let go of resentments and embrace forgiveness as a powerful tool for positive change.

One of the biggest obstacles to self-forgiveness is the belief that we must be perfect in order to be worthy of forgiveness. This belief is often fuelled by society's emphasis on achievement and success, and the pressure to present a flawless image to the world. However, this idea of perfection is an illusion that can prevent us from healing and moving forward. In this chapter, we will explore the importance of forgiving yourself for not being perfect and provide practical tips for letting go of self-judgment and self-criticism.

The Problem with Perfectionism

Perfectionism is a common trait among individuals who struggle with self-forgiveness. Perfectionists hold themselves to impossibly high standards, which often lead to feelings of guilt, shame, and self-blame when they fall short of their goals. They believe that mistakes are unacceptable and equate them with failure, leading to a constant cycle of self-criticism and negative self-talk. This mind-set can be especially damaging when it comes to forgiveness because it can prevent individuals from extending compassion and understanding to themselves.

Why It's Okay to Be Imperfect

The truth is that no one is perfect. We all make mistakes, experience setbacks, and face challenges throughout our lives. It's important to remember that making mistakes is a natural part of the learning process, and we often grow and learn the most from our failures. Additionally, the expectation of perfection is unrealistic and sets us up for disappointment and self-doubt. Embracing our imperfections allows us to cultivate self-compassion and self-acceptance, which are essential components of self-forgiveness.

Steps toward Self-Forgiveness

Recognize your inner critic: The first step towards self-forgiveness is to become aware of your inner critic. Notice the negative self-talk and judgments that arise when you make a mistake or fall short of your goals. Recognize that these thoughts are not helpful or productive and only serve to reinforce feelings of guilt and shame.

Challenge your beliefs: The next step is to challenge the belief that you must be perfect in order to be worthy of forgiveness. Reflect on where this belief comes from and how it has influenced your thoughts and behaviours. Replace these limiting beliefs with positive affirmations that acknowledge your worth and value, regardless of your mistakes.

Practice self-compassion: Cultivate self-compassion by treating yourself with kindness and understanding. Remember that everyone makes mistakes, and that it's okay to be imperfect. Practice self-care and engage in activities that bring you joy and comfort.

Learn from your mistakes: Instead of dwelling on your mistakes, use them as an opportunity for growth and learning. Reflect on what you can do differently in the future and use this knowledge to make positive changes in your life.

Let go of the past: Holding onto past mistakes only prolongs feelings of guilt and shame. Let go of the past and focus on the present moment. Forgive yourself for any perceived wrongdoings and commit to moving forward with a positive mind-set.

Conclusion

Forgiving yourself for not being perfect is a crucial step towards self-forgiveness and healing. It requires acknowledging the harmful effects of perfectionism and embracing our imperfections with self-compassion and understanding. By challenging negative beliefs, practicing self-care, and learning from our mistakes, we can let go of self-judgment and move towards a more positive and fulfilling life. Remember that forgiveness is a process, and it takes time and patience to cultivate a mind-set of self-love and acceptance.

Moving Forward After Forgiveness

Forgiveness is a powerful tool that can help us release negative emotions, let go of resentment, and find peace within ourselves. But once we have forgiven, what comes next? How can we move forward in our lives, free from the burden of past hurts and pain?

In this chapter, we will explore the ways in which we can continue to grow and thrive after forgiveness, and how we can use this newfound sense of freedom to create positive change in our lives.

Embracing a Positive Mind-set

After forgiveness, it's important to focus on the positive aspects of life. A positive mind-set can help us stay motivated, resilient, and optimistic, even in the face of challenges. It's important to remember that forgiveness is not the end of the journey, but rather the beginning of a new one. By adopting a positive outlook, we can open ourselves up to new opportunities, new relationships, and new experiences.

One way to cultivate a positive mind-set is to focus on gratitude. By acknowledging and expressing gratitude for the good things in our lives, we can shift our focus away from negativity and towards the positive. Whether it's the love and support of friends and family, the beauty of nature, or the simple pleasures of life, there is always something to be thankful for. By taking the time to appreciate these things, we can cultivate a sense of happiness and contentment that can help us move forward with confidence.

Setting Goals and Taking Action

Once we have forgiven, it's important to set goals and take action towards achieving them. By setting realistic goals and taking concrete steps towards achieving them, we can regain a sense of control over our lives and move forward with purpose. This could involve pursuing a new career, starting a new hobby, or simply making positive changes to our daily routine.

It's important to remember that moving forward doesn't necessarily mean forgetting the past. We can still acknowledge and learn from our past experiences, while at the same time embracing the present and looking towards the future. By taking proactive steps towards our goals, we can create a sense of momentum that can help us overcome any obstacles in our path.

Finding Support

Forgiveness can be a challenging process, and it's important to have a support system in place to help us navigate the ups and downs of the journey. Whether it's the support of friends and family, a therapist or counsellor, or a support group, having people in our lives who understand what we've been through can be incredibly helpful.

It's important to remember that healing is not a linear process, and that setbacks and challenges are a natural part of the journey. By having a support system in place, we can get the encouragement, guidance, and emotional support we need to keep moving forward.

Practicing Self-Care

Finally, after forgiveness, it's important to prioritize self-care. This means taking care of our physical, emotional, and mental health by getting enough sleep, eating a healthy diet, exercising regularly, and taking time for activities that bring us joy and relaxation.

Self-care is not a luxury, but rather a necessity for our overall well-being. By taking care of ourselves, we can reduce stress, improve our mood, and increase our overall sense of well-being. This can help us stay focused and motivated as we continue to move forward after forgiveness.

In conclusion, forgiveness is a powerful tool that can help us release negative emotions and find peace within ourselves. But it's just the beginning of a new journey, and moving forward after forgiveness requires effort and commitment. By embracing a positive mind-set, setting goals and taking action, finding support, and practicing self-care, we can continue to grow and thrive after forgiveness, and create a life that is full of joy, purpose, and meaning.

Printed by BoD [illegible], Germany

9 789357 333511